T0114651

BLADES OF ELOQUENCE

The Power of Logos in the Duel of Words

Caroline Hanna Guirgis

WESTBOW
PRESS®
A DIVISION OF THOMAS NELSON
& ZONDERVAN

WestBow Press books may be ordered through booksellers or by contacting:

WestBow Press
A Division of Thomas Nelson & Zondervan
1663 Liberty Drive
Bloomington, IN 47403
www.westbowpress.com
844-714-3454

ISBN: 979-8-3850-0935-0 (sc)
ISBN: 979-8-3850-0937-4 (hc)
ISBN: 979-8-3850-0936-7 (e)

Library of Congress Control Number: 2023919224

Print information available on the last page.

WestBow Press rev. date: 10/12/2023

Contents

Dedication

To Mark, my steadfast anchor, with whom I've journeyed through three transformative decades. His profound insights were my first window into the essence of heartfelt communication. As our bond deepened in joyful and challenging moments, Mark revealed the intricate alchemy of words—their ability to heal and hurt. Without our shared path, the nuanced power of words might have remained a mystery, and beyond that, the deep resonance of The Word, The Logos. When words lose their essence and resonance, I discovered the sacred lexicon bestowed upon me through the Divine's Son, the Logos. Yet, mastering such a celestial tongue is no trifling pursuit.

May this tome mark the dawn of everyone's quest to uncover the profound essence of the WORD, transcending the everyday utterances that often deprive us of truth, honor, and love. Let's endeavor to see beyond our mere words, seeking instead those that uplift, heal, and inspire change. Together, may our words and actions radiate truth in love.

Introduction

A few things hold as much power and charisma as words. They are not just combinations of letters or sounds but vessels of emotion, history, culture, and thought, bridging the gap between souls and shaping civilizations' narratives. Words carry personal legacies, tales of joy, sorrow, love, and mystery for everyone. They define comfort and challenge and become beacons of our deepest desires and fears. Language has evolved alongside humanity, with each word embodying a universe of contexts, nuances, and histories. But where does the definition of a word originate? Is it in the dusty scrolls of ancient civilizations, the resonating proclamations of great leaders, or the hushed whispers between lovers?

Join me on a journey exploring words, understanding their significance, and uncovering their cultural origins. Through this exploration, we hope not just to understand words but also the intricate tapestry of human emotion and history they weave. Words are not merely sequences of letters strung together; they pulsate with life and vigor. Each word, whether whispered or proclaimed boldly, holds within it an undeniable power—a force potent enough to inspire, heal, hurt, motivate, or transform. Once spoken or written, words take on a life of their own, traveling across hearts and minds, shaping thoughts, and influencing decisions. They can be as nurturing as a mother's lullaby or as destructive as a storm, reflecting their profound impact on human emotions and actions. Revolutions are birthed, love is kindled, and souls are mended through the resonance of words. Every utterance, every penned line, has the potential to change a person's trajectory, reminding us of the living legacy and transformative power embedded in our words.

The relationship between words and communication is deeply intertwined, with words serving as the foundation for effective communication. They are essential tools through which individuals express their thoughts, ideas, emotions, and information to others. The correlation is intricate, as the use of words enables shared understanding, clarity, and precision in communication. The right words convey information, persuade, influence, and narrate stories while allowing for expressing emotions and transmitting cultural values. Furthermore, words are pivotal in problem-solving, relationship-building, and fostering innovation. They are the linchpin of human interaction, facilitating knowledge exchange, connecting people, and enriching our ability to comprehend and connect with the world.

Within the pages of this book, you will uncover a deeper understanding of the significance and impact held within the words we choose. Yet, amidst this intricate tapestry of language, a paramount revelation exists: the ultimate importance of a single, final word. Through this exploration, you will grasp the profound truth that while every word carries its significance, there exists One Word that holds the utmost power and resonance.

1

Words as Weapons

My brother, sister and I had taken this route countless times, the familiar path that connected our school to the sanctuary of our home. But on this day, the air around us seemed to tremble with tension, like the silent moments before a storm. It began as a murmur, distant and almost inaudible. Then, hurried footsteps grew louder, echoing ominously off the surrounding buildings. Before we could fully grasp the situation, a group of kids' faces contorted with anger and malice surrounded us. The shadows they cast seemed to merge with the growing darkness. "We heard you're Egyptians," spat out one of them, his voice dripping with venom. I recall the confusion and doubt that raced through my mind.

What did our Egyptian heritage have to do with anything?

It didn't take long for their fury to become clear: the Iran hostage situation of the 1980s. A geopolitical crisis thousands of miles away had, inconceivably, placed us in the eye of a local storm. The irony was cruel; we were not even Iranian. But to these kids, blinded by ignorance and prejudice, we were 'the other,' a convenient target for their misplaced rage. My brother bore the brunt of their fury. Punches were thrown, kicks landed, and their words—hurtful, vile—pierced deeper than any physical blow. "Terrorist," they screamed, "Go back home!" Each syllable was a dagger, revealing a new, painful truth: words could be lethal weapons.

Tears blurred my vision, but my ears couldn't escape the hate-filled chants. My brother's pleas, my screams, and the vicious taunts of our attackers melded into a cacophony of pain and prejudice. We were left shaken, bruised, and forever changed when it was over. The physical wounds would heal, but the scars left by their words—those remained, etched into our souls. From that day, I recognized the raw, destructive power of words. Misinformation, prejudice, and ignorance have transformed everyday words into missiles, targeting our identities.

The journey home was a blur. Our once-familiar path now seemed treacherous and hostile. But as the days turned into weeks and weeks into months, a determination grew within me. I resolved to understand the true power of words, to wield them not as weapons of hate but as tools for change, understanding, and unity. But I was too angry.

As the eldest, merely in the 6th grade, I felt an overwhelming responsibility to protect my younger siblings. That evening, our battered spirits chose silence. We concealed our bruises, swallowed our tears, and never let our parents glimpse the horrors we had endured. But within me, a fire was kindling. I couldn't, wouldn't, let this happen again. Life, however, has its plans. Not long after, history threatened to repeat itself on another seemingly ordinary day. The same hateful eyes began their dance of intimidation. But this time, something had shifted in me. With the memories of that traumatic day still fresh and my brother and sister looking at me, I stood tall, summoning a courage I didn't know I had. Drawing a deep breath, I unleashed my arsenal: words.

"Enough!" I thundered, stepping between the bullies and my siblings. "We have as much right to be here as you do. Your ignorance does not define us. We are proud of our heritage, and your misplaced hatred won't change that." My voice held a fierceness, a determination that took them by surprise. Every word I hurled was a shield, a barrier against their prejudice. It wasn't a magical solution; words alone rarely are. But in that moment, I discovered their true power. Yes, they could hurt, but they could also heal, protect, and defy. From that day on, I vowed to harness this power, turning words from weapons of harm into instruments of change.

While the idealist in me had once hoped to use words to educate and heal, reality had sculpted them into a weapon for me. Again, I found myself fiercely wielding them to defend my siblings, my friends, and any innocent soul that crossed paths with ignorance or cruelty. They became my tool, shield, and, when necessary, my sword. Though I had dreamt of a world where words could solely be instruments of change and understanding, I realized that sometimes they needed to be weapons first to protect and fight against injustice. Only then could they pave the way for the more significant, profound change I had once envisioned.

As days turned weeks and weeks into months, confrontations with the group of bullies became a part of our routine. But within the school's walls, I had my nemesis: a tall, imposing 8th-grader named Keisha. Her dark skin seemed to absorb the harsh overhead lights of our school hallways, and her eyes, always fierce, frequently found their way to me. Keisha would jeer at me, push past me in corridors, and sometimes spill my books from my hands. Initially, I saw her actions as a continuation of the hatred I faced outside school. But as days wore on, I began to see beneath the surface. Despite her aggressive front towards me, I saw her face her bullies. Whispers of "too dark," "ugly," and other cruel jibes would follow her, a constant, haunting soundtrack.

It dawned on me that Keisha's aggression wasn't indeed about me. It was a defense mechanism, a way for her to regain some control in a world where she felt cornered because of her skin color. Recognizing this shared struggle, a shift began in me. Rather than seeing her as an adversary, I began empathizing with her pain, anger, and need to assert herself. One day, as a particularly nasty group of girls cornered Keisha, I stepped in without thinking. "Leave her alone," I declared, surprising myself with my assertiveness. The girls, taken aback by my intervention, hesitated, allowing Keisha and me to lock eyes briefly. In that split second, an understanding passed between us. We were both victims, caught in a storm of prejudice, trying to navigate our way while protecting ourselves.

From that day on, our relationship began to change. The hallway confrontations ceased, and while we weren't fast friends, we became unexpected allies. We understood each other's battles and often found ourselves defending not just ourselves but each other. Through Keisha, I learned that sometimes the line between bully and victim is blurred, and the key to breaking the cycle is understanding and compassion.

2

The Unlikely Warrior

There's a vast chasm between the child I was at home and the protector I became outside of it. At home, I was the picture of obedience, the compliant child who nodded in agreement, never raising my voice or daring to challenge my parents. My natural disposition was calm, always keen on blending in rather than standing out. To those who knew me intimately, I was a gentle soul who wouldn't even harm a fly. And yet, faced with a threat to my loved ones, something primal, almost otherworldly, awakened within me. Where did this reservoir of courage come from? How did a child who'd never uttered a word in defiance at home find the strength to stand up to bullies on the street, defending her siblings and others in the line of prejudice?

Years later, during a chance reunion, I met with those very

tormentors from our childhood. Time had softened their edges, and remorse shone clearly in their eyes. What they confessed took me by surprise. "You know," one of them began hesitantly, "we never expected words like those from someone like you. You caught us off guard, truly." Another said, "It wasn't just the words; it was how you said them. With such conviction, such authority. It felt like you weren't just a kid anymore, but someone who commanded respect." Hearing this, memories flooded back, reminding me of that pivotal moment when I had transformed from a passive observer to an active defender. My words, fueled by an innate desire to protect and shield, had not only startled them but had also evoked a sense of respect.

Life is replete with mysteries; perhaps one of mine was this inexplicable metamorphosis. But in those moments, when loved ones were in jeopardy, I was reminded of a fundamental truth: within each of us, often buried deep beneath layers of conditioning and societal expectations, lies an indomitable spirit ready to rise in defense of justice and love. Life is often a juxtaposition of contrasting beliefs and behaviors, and I was no exception to this rule. While fiercely championing justice and fairness in the outside world, I was haunted by the knowledge of my imperfections. Why was there this chasm between who I was and who I aspired to be? Why did I demand of the world what I sometimes couldn't uphold within myself?

I recall instances where I'd snapped at a sibling for a trivial matter or held onto petty grudges. I'd been unjust in moments of frustration and sometimes lacked the fairness I adamantly expected from others. And yet, whenever I witnessed blatant prejudice or cruelty, a fire would ignite within me, pushing me to combat these injustices. It was this very recognition of my flaws that intensified my drive. It might have been an unspoken yearning to balance the scales for the world and my soul. By fiercely advocating for righteousness in the external world, I may be trying to atone for or reconcile with the lapses in my character.

It's also possible that I understood that the world doesn't function absolutely in all its complexity. Having flaws doesn't negate one's right or duty to fight for what's right. Often, our imperfections make us most human, allowing us to empathize, understand, and ultimately take a stand. Over time, I learned to embrace this paradox within me. While I continued to strive for personal growth and self-improvement, I also accepted that my internal battles didn't diminish the validity or intensity of the external ones. If anything, they made my fight more genuine, grounded in the understanding that the journey towards justice and fairness is a collective effort, fraught with imperfections but always worth pursuing.

Respect was a cornerstone of my upbringing, a value deeply embedded in the very fabric of my being. No matter the person's age, background, or circumstance, I inherently believed in treating them with dignity. Each interaction, from fleeting exchanges with strangers to deep conversations with loved ones, carried this undercurrent of reverence for the human spirit. However, my respect for individuals never closed my eyes to the injustices they might perpetrate or experience. Whenever unfairness loomed, I felt a visceral urge to intervene. My approach, though, needed to be more monolithic. It morphed, fluidly adapting to the context and intensity of the situation.

There were moments when a gentle word, a bridge of

9

understanding, was enough to diffuse tensions and highlight the injustice. Sometimes, a simple conversation, layered with empathy and reason, could pave the way for change. But then some situations demanded more. When faced with blatant prejudice or malicious intent, I stepped in with a forcefulness that surprised even me. Whether it was confronting a bully who targeted someone weaker or challenging discriminatory remarks, I found myself using every ounce of my strength and conviction to battle injustice. Yet, the intent was never mere confrontation for confrontation's sake. Even in my most aggressive interventions, there was a purpose: to illuminate the wrong, to make the perpetrator reflect, and to uplift the downtrodden. The methods varied - sometimes it was a forcefully articulated argument, other times a silent yet defiant stand. But the underpinning remained the same: a relentless pursuit of justice using fighting words.

Reflecting upon these moments, I recognized that my reactions weren't merely about addressing the situation. They were a testament to my deep-seated belief in a world where fairness wasn't a luxury but a right. A world where, despite my imperfections, I could play a role, however small, in inching us closer to that ideal.

Among the various forms of unfairness and prejudice I encountered, one behavior tested my patience and resolve more than others: passive aggressiveness. While overt hostility was easy to pinpoint and address, passive-aggressiveness was a different beast, cloaked in ambiguity and often leaving a trail of confusion. Dealing with passive-aggressiveness felt like navigating a labyrinth without a clear map. The offhand comments laden with underlying spite, the thinly veiled jabs disguised as innocent observations, and the deliberate exclusion masked as an oversight. These instances were needles in the haystack, often harder to identify but causing disproportionate distress.

What irked me the most was the cowardice inherent in such actions. It felt like a way to inflict pain without having the courage to be straightforward about one's feelings or intentions. And it wasn't just the deceit that bothered me. With its subtle underpinnings, passive aggressiveness made its victims doubt their perceptions and emotions, questioning whether they were overreacting or misinterpreting. Each time I encountered this behavior, I felt torn. My natural inclination to address injustices head-on clashed with the elusive nature of passive-aggressiveness. Confronting it directly often seemed like granting the perpetrator what they wanted – a reaction. Yet, letting it slide felt like an endorsement of this toxic behavior.

I wanted to develop a strategy and a middle ground. I tried to call out the behavior, not with aggression but with open-ended questions, seeking clarity. "Did you mean... when you said...?" or "I felt a bit sidelined when this happened; was that the intention?" Doing so would put the onus on the other person to either confront their actions or clarify their intentions. This approach would not be about confrontation for its own sake but an attempt to bring transparency to ambiguous situations. It could be my way of reaffirming that, while I might grapple with my imperfections, I wouldn't allow underhanded tactics to erode the respect and fairness I so ardently championed.

However, it wasn't always a clear path when dealing with passive-aggressiveness. In truth, for years, I tolerated it, not entirely grasping its insidious nature. On the surface, these encounters seemed like minor irritations, but they were quickly brushed aside. But like water dripping on a stone, the continuous exposure eroded my self-assuredness. At first, I scarcely noticed the change. But over time, I second-guessed my judgments, reevaluated conversations in my head, and agonized over the real intent behind seemingly benign comments. This silent, psychological warfare differed from the overt confrontations I was used to. The battle wasn't out in the open; it was within me, an internal struggle where I was both the defender and the one needing defense.

I had internalized the doubt and ambiguity inherent in passive-aggressive interactions without realizing it. This had a cascading effect. My usual decisiveness began to waver. My voice once rang clear and assertively, occasionally trembling with uncertainty. The words that had been my shield and sword in the face of blatant aggression now sometimes failed me when navigating these murky waters. It took considerable introspection to recognize the toll it was taking on me. And with that realization came another: while I had honed my skills at confronting overt injustice, I had left myself vulnerable to the more covert, veiled kind. Recognizing this was my first step towards reclaiming my voice and sense of self. The journey back to self-assuredness could have been swifter and more linear. It involved setting boundaries, seeking support, and relearning to trust my instincts. But it was a necessary journey, reaffirming that the fight for fairness isn't just against external adversaries but, sometimes, against the doubts and fears sown within.

3

The Reflection and Reckoning

2017 marked a turning point, a moment of profound introspection. It was as if a mirror was held up to me, revealing not just the protector and champion of fairness I had been but also the times I had misused that power. In certain situations, the very weapon I had wielded in defense of others had turned into an instrument of offense. Strangely, this recklessness manifested more prominently in my Christian communities, where I should have been a beacon of love, understanding, and compassion. Why was this happening? How could I become a source of discord in places that should epitomize grace? With each confrontation, words, once my trusted allies, betrayed me. They rushed out, unchecked, raw, and sometimes scathing. The aftermath of these exchanges often left me bewildered, regretful, and laden with guilt. My actions seemed paradoxical. Why was I more confrontational, even aggressive, towards those who shared my faith, the very cornerstone of my being, than with those outside this fold?

As I delved deeper, I understood the layers of expectations and pressures within faith communities. There was an unspoken standard, a behavior, belief, and thought benchmark. And when I perceived deviations or inconsistencies, my instinctual drive for fairness was triggered. But this time, it was exacerbated by spiritual disappointment and heightened expectations. If we, as believers, couldn't get it right, then who could? This mindset and my inherent desire for justice created a potent mix, making me react more forcefully than warranted. Acknowledging this pattern was both humbling and painful. I realized that in my zeal for upholding righteousness within my faith community, I had sometimes forgotten the core of our belief – grace, mercy, and love. My aggressive approach was, in many ways, antithetical to the teachings of Christ, who emphasized understanding, forgiveness, and gentle correction.

It was a period of soul-searching, of reevaluating my motivations and methods. I embarked on a journey of self-correction, leaning into the very tenets of faith I felt I had drifted from. I aimed to recalibrate my approach through prayer, reflection, and seeking counsel. My goal shifted from being just a defender of fairness to becoming a conduit of grace, understanding that actual change, especially within faith communities, comes from embodying the principles of love and kindness rather than sheer confrontation.

Some moments in life stand out, not necessarily for their significance in the grand tapestry of events, but for the raw emotions they evoke. One such episode occurred when I found myself face to face with my superior, a person I deeply respected and looked up to. The backdrop of this confrontation wasn't just any disagreement but a painful realization that he had placed his trust in slander rather than drawing from his God-given wisdom. I was incensed. The weight of the betrayal, the sting of others being judged based on hearsay rather than firsthand knowledge, triggered a reaction more volatile than I could have anticipated. Before I knew it, words erupted, fierce and unfiltered. My voice, usually modulated and composed, rose to a shout, each word echoing my pain, disappointment, and sheer disbelief.

When the dust settled, a heavy silence ensued. The immediacy of the confrontation was overshadowed by a more profound, gnawing pain. It wasn't just about the external conflict but the internal turmoil that followed. I was distraught, not just because of the accusations or the broken trust but because of my reaction. For days, I wrestled with the consequences. How could I, an advocate for the potency of words, have let them spill out so thoughtlessly? Why did I allow my feelings to erupt in a situation that required composure and discernment? The irony wasn't lost on me; the very words that I believed in that I had used as shields and weapons had turned against me. And more so, against someone in a leadership position within my faith community. I was drained. It felt like the very essence that fueled my spirit had been depleted. The frustration was twofold: anger at the unfairness of the situation and a more resounding disappointment in myself. How had I allowed my emotions to overshadow the principles I held dear?

As days turned to weeks, this incident became a pivotal moment of introspection. I recognized that while seeking justice and fairness was a noble endeavor, it had to be balanced with grace, humility, and restraint. After all, isn't that what my faith taught? To "speak the truth in love," to "be quick to listen, slow to speak, and slow to become angry." It was a lesson in humility and growth. I had faltered, but it paved the way for reconciliation with my superior and myself. The journey ahead would be learning, recognizing the thin line between passion and impulsiveness, and continually striving to align my actions with the principles of love, grace, and wisdom.

No matter how personal, every story draws from a tapestry woven long before its narrator's birth. My quest to understand words' immense power didn't just stem from personal experiences but also from an insatiable thirst for wisdom. I delved deep to grasp words' weight, tracing their origin and evolution. And in doing so, I found myself returning to the very foundation of my faith: the Bible.

The Tower of Babel, as described in the Book of Genesis, is a profound metaphor for the power and pitfalls of human communication. A united humanity, speaking a single language, sought to construct a tower that reached the heavens. Their motive, rooted in ambition, showcased the sheer force of unified communication. They believed, with one voice and purpose, that nothing they planned would be impossible for them. But this monumental endeavor was not met with divine approval. Instead, it was perceived as a challenge to the religious order, a testament to humanity's hubris. In response, God confounded their speech, ensuring they could no longer understand one another. This divine act, scattering them across the Earth, effectively halted their collective project.

This ancient Biblical account offers a duality in its lesson. On one hand, it's a testament to the formidable power of words and unified communication. Humans can accomplish monumental feats when they speak the same language and have a shared purpose. But on the other hand, it's a cautionary story about the dangers of unchecked ambition and the potential consequences of miscommunication. The Tower of Babel is not just about linguistic diversity; it encapsulates the eternal connection between cooperation and conflict, unity and division. It serves as a reminder that words can divide as much as they can unite. And when misused or misunderstood, they can lead to confusion, chaos, and disarray.

Drawing from this biblical chronicle, I began to see the parallels in my life. Just as the builders of Babel experienced the might and mishaps of communication, so had I. Words were my bridge and my barrier. They connected me to others, supported causes, and defended the vulnerable. Yet, they were also the source of conflict, pain, and personal regret. The Tower of Babel became a lens through which I viewed my journey. It helped me appreciate the balance required in harnessing the power of words: to respect their potential, to wield them responsibly, and to recognize the thin line when good meets bad in communication.

As I write the following chapters, I hope readers, too, can reflect on the words they utter, the bridges they build, and the towers they might unknowingly be constructing. Because, in words, we find the essence of our shared humanity: our aspirations, our flaws, and our eternal quest for understanding.

4

Unleashing the Power

At the beginning of my journey lies a profound exploration of the potency inherent in words. Unaware of their might, the words I once harnessed possessed the potential to wound, divide, and create chaos. Like a double-edged sword, my language could cut through the hearts of others, leaving scars that lingered.

Yet, with time, a transformation began to unfold. A pivotal realization emerged—that these words, once handled recklessly, could be harnessed for a nobler purpose. The journey took shape from wielding words as a lethal arsenal to using them as resolution tools. It involved delving into the art of conflict resolution, learning to navigate disagreements with empathy, and seeking common ground amid diverse perspectives. This chapter delves into the heart of this transformation—an exploration of understanding, compassion, and the quest to mend the breaches that my words had once created.

The journey toward manipulating words with intention and positivity marked a crucial juncture. It involved consciously choosing words that uplifted, inspired, and healed. This chapter unravels the endeavor—a commitment to creating a symphony of positivity in spoken and unspoken expressions. It's a narrative woven with the threads of mindfulness as I embraced the power to shape interactions that kindled warmth, understanding, and unity. Each chapter of this journey led to the culmination of a newfound mastery—the ability to use words correctly, responsibly, and effectively. It was an expedition through introspection and growth, an odyssey that demanded the discernment of knowing when to speak and when to listen.

In tracing this narrative arc from a lethal arsenal of words to the mastery of positive and effective communication, this book unravels growth, self-awareness, and transformation. It's a journey that weaves through conflict, resolution, and the aspiration to use words as tools for healing, connection, and the elevation of human experience. In the moment of utterance, before conscious thought had its say, I recognized the potency of my words. It was not precision that guided them but the imperfect musings of my mind. My preoccupation was not with the impact of my words upon the listener's soul but with the urgency to release them, imparting lessons no one had sought from me.

A storm of toxic thoughts brewed in the shadowed recesses of my mind. Like a river tainted at its source, these turbulent musings flowed into my words, casting an evil hue upon them. The more I voiced these words, the more they became an indelible part of my essence, tainting not just my speech but the core of my being. In the face of the Divine, the weight of my words became unmistakably clear. Set against God's profound truths, my utterances seemed feeble and marred. Even my prayers, which should have been sanctuaries of humility and grace, were tinged with the bitterness of judgment and condemnation.

But it was in this stark contrast that I began to recognize the disparity. The very act of measuring my words against God's revealed to me the need for transformation, a genuine yearning to cleanse the wellspring of my thoughts and, in turn, purify the words that flowed forth. With profound remorse, I reflect on what I believed was my shield and sword. That which I once wielded against others turned inwards, making me its prime target. These treacherous thoughts and words, intended to safeguard, only ensnared me, laying the foundation for fractured relationships. In my hubris (a Greek-origin word that refers to excessive pride or self-confidence, often to the point of arrogance. In classical Greek literature, hubris often leads to a downfall or punishment. It signifies an overestimation of one's competence or capabilities, especially when the person exhibiting it thinks they are in a position of power). I was constructing my Tower of Babel (Babel means "to confuse"), blind to the impending downfall it promised.

Words can be healing tools in the sanctity of prayer and the solace of shared burdens. Yet, when carried out without care, they can morph into barriers. For example, in the sacred bond of marriage, how can one beleaguered by abuse summon the strength to pray for the transformation of the soul that inflicts pain upon them? To expect such transcendence of hurt in pursuit of another's spiritual salvation might seem unfathomable in contemporary discourse. Today, many have lost the ability to recognize the underlying causes of their spouse's pain. Instead of understanding and healing, our choice of harsh and condemning words often fuels the flames, further damaging an already fragile spirit.

Reflecting upon my brother's journey, where addiction veiled his vision and silenced his voice, I discerned a parallel captivity in my soul. Though chains of addiction did not tether me, chains of pride did, making me believe in the grandeur of my own words. Even in my prayers, I prioritized eloquence over earnestness, forsaking the true essence of communion with the Divine.

As John's sister, I stood witness to a transformation that defied all expectations—a journey of redemption fueled by the living Word I couldn't fathom when all other avenues had failed. Our shared history was woven with memories of a childhood immersed in the teachings of faith, yet life's twists and turns led my brother down a path of addiction, a battle that seemed impossible. The Word that had once kindled his spirit appeared to fade amidst the darkness of addiction, leaving me questioning how such divine guidance could reach him amid his struggles. Despite my doubts, John's story unfolded as an astonishing testament to the profound impact of the living Word. Those early encounters with the sacred teachings, which had seemed forgotten, became the foundation on which he rebuilt his life. The Word had persevered in his heart, its messages of hope, healing, and redemption echoing even in his darkest moments. His journey from the depths of addiction to a life of triumph was not just a personal victory but a revelation of the Word's enduring power to uplift and transform.

Through the recovery process, John unearthed the strength that had lain dormant within him, fueled by the timeless wisdom of the living Word. It was as though the sacred stories reached through the haze of addiction, beckoning him toward renewal. With each scripture he revisited, he found solace, guidance, and the resilience to break free from the chains that bound him. The living Word, which had seemed distant, became a lifeline guiding him back to the light.

John's triumph over addiction is a testament to the living Word's capacity to inspire renewal despite seemingly insurmountable challenges. Once marked by despair, his journey was now a beacon of hope and healing. As his sister, I learned that the divine guidance we couldn't fathom held the power to redeem and transform beyond our comprehension. John's story illuminates that circumstances do not confine the living Word's messages of grace, love, and redemption; they possess the timeless ability to rekindle the human spirit and guide us from darkness into the radiance of new beginnings.

5

The Unforeseen Redemption

In our society, the adage "hurt people hurt people" often becomes a self-perpetuating cycle, and breaking free without inflicting further pain is a challenge. While I acknowledge that divorces happen and sometimes are inevitable, it's not my place to pass judgment, as I don't know the intricacies of individual stories. Yet, irrespective of the reasons or circumstances, this cycle of pain often perpetuates into the following generations. It leads many to question whether enduring an unloving marriage might be preferable to ending it. However, the worldly concept of love doesn't truly encapsulate the essence of marriage.

God, the embodiment of unconditional love, epitomizes true foundational love. Our human understanding and capacity for love pale in comparison to God's love—a love so profound that it led to the sacrifice of His Son. God remains committed to His people, even when they turn away from Him. The ultimate question is, would we be willing to make similar sacrifices for our spouse? Can we find it within ourselves to pray for someone, even if they've deeply hurt us? It's worth reflecting on.

Reflecting on the fragile tapestry of modern matrimonial bonds, seeing love morph into animosity is perplexing. How do soulmates dissipate into voids? Do lifelong confidantes transform into adversaries? Co-guardians of life's most precious gifts metamorphose into distant silhouettes? Could it be that mere words create this chasm? Do they wield such formidable might? The words that once signified eternal commitment now herald the demise of unions, as "till death do us part" becomes an echoing lament of love lost. In one breath, you declared an eternal love, and in the very next, tears of hatred flowed.

The declaration "I hate you" often stems from complex emotions, experiences, and situations, making its root cause multifaceted. One primary trigger is emotional overwhelm. People might resort to such potent language in intense anger, frustration, or sadness, even if their underlying feelings aren't hatred. This statement can also emerge from feelings of vulnerability. When individuals feel hurt, rejected, or threatened, they might use it as a defensive mechanism to protect themselves or create emotional distance. Additionally, past traumas and unresolved issues can inadvertently manifest in such expressions, primarily if they haven't been adequately addressed. It's crucial to understand that while the words might seem clear-cut, the emotions and reasons driving them can be deeply intricate.

Why have our words taken precedence over those of the Divine, especially when we are vessels of His spirit? We, who discern right from wrong, wisdom from folly, and truth from deceit, have become heedless. Why do we allow sacred words to be tainted with vulgarity? Why do we stand by as human adjudicators sever unions sanctified by God? Why do we let the words of others dictate our being, and why do we remain silent in the face of truth, especially when falsehoods proliferate unchecked?

Why do I focus primarily on marriage?

The very fabric of society, which is interwoven with relationships, trust, and mutual understanding, starts to unravel when marriages break down. On the other hand, the second reason emphasizes personal growth and self-awareness. Understanding oneself, pursuing personal passions, and achieving individual milestones are essential before entering a partnership. A solid, unique form is the cornerstone of a strong relationship. When two people who clearly understand themselves come together, the chances of a thriving and resilient union increase manifold. Therefore, whether you prioritize marriage or personal growth, the aim should be to create a foundation of understanding, love, and respect for the institution of marriage or oneself.

When will we draw the line? What will catalyze us to stand together to defend the truth, champion the vulnerable, and maintain our ethical standards? Where can we seek solace and illumination if our utterances breed despair and cast shadows?

We are presented with choices in the face of marital discord.

In the first option, we perpetuate a cycle of pain and resentment. We spotlight our spouse's imperfections, vocalize their misdeeds, and surround ourselves with allies who reinforce negative perceptions. This alienates our partner and fuels the inner turmoil they may be grappling with, providing it with the proverbial "junk food" it craves, leading to an endless loop of negativity. For those of faith, it's essential to recognize that the battle isn't necessarily against our spouse but against the harmful spirit influencing them. However, reciprocating malice only serves to amplify it.

On the other hand, we are left pondering how to cope with our anguish, particularly when faced with adversity or mistreatment within the marriage. Every relationship is unique, and circumstances can differ widely. The answer is clear when personal safety is at risk: distance oneself and seek refuge. However, this message is particularly tailored for couples who feel their love has dimmed or has drifted apart. In these instances, reflection, communication, and mutual understanding become paramount.

Our second choice, undeniably more challenging, requires assistance beyond human capability. When Jesus ascended, leaving his disciples, he left behind teachings and a promise he fulfilled. He bequeathed them the Holy Spirit, the Comforter. This divine spirit, bestowed upon believers, provides discernment, peace, and the strength required to face challenges that might seem impossible. I wish to emphasize the gravity of this journey. Despite considering myself a strong, independent individual with a command over words, they only served to amplify my rage and diminish my faith. Instead of leaning into the Spirit of Jesus within me, I relegated it to the background, prioritizing control over surrender. This choice led me into profound darkness.

Please heed my words when I assert that unchecked anger can be devastating when separated from God's guiding spirit. It's not that God prohibits anger; indeed, He acknowledges it. However, He commands us, "In your anger, do not sin." This statement might initially seem paradoxical, but it unveils deep wisdom upon reflection. The Bible contains this guidance not as a contradiction but as an insightful observation of the human condition. It acknowledges our emotions but cautions against allowing them to lead us astray.

So, the pressing question arises: what is our course of action? Should we resign ourselves to being passive or submissive? The answer is a resounding 'no'. Christians are neither feeble nor are they to be trampled upon. Our strength lies in the very essence of our creation and purpose. We must immerse ourselves in the Living Word of God, making it our shield and sword in the spiritual battles we face. Every verse every scripture we read in the Bible is not just text but a transformative power. By internalizing and living out the Word, we allow it to saturate our hearts, govern our thoughts, and influence our reactions. In doing so, the Spirit's power unveils the true nature of the conflict: recognizing that our dear ones are trapped by their pain and wounds.

In these trying moments, our refuge and sustenance come from the Word of God. It's not merely about reading it but about soaking it in, reflecting upon it, and letting it nurture our spirits. This Word becomes our solace, declaration, proclamation, and anchor. When faced with adversities, we hold fast to this Word, reminding ourselves of God's promises, power, and unwavering love.

When scripture advises believers to "speak to one another in Psalms," it is typically seen in a communal and worshipful context. This directive is found in the New Testament, in Ephesians 5:19, which states: "Speaking to one another with psalms, hymns, and songs from the Spirit. Sing and make music from your heart to the Lord." The implications and interpretations of this instruction are manifold.

Historically, in liturgical worship, many Christian traditions have woven the Psalms into their practices, either reciting or singing them as part of their communal devotion. Emphasizing hymns of praise and laments, the Psalms act as sources of comfort, hope, and encouragement. When believers share these verses, they uplift and enlighten their peers. By regularly speaking and singing the Psalms, believers also internalize the Word of God, embedding it in their daily lives and thoughts. Furthermore, considering the Psalms as prayers, articulating or singing them becomes a form of collective prayer or a means to convey individual petitions to God. Engaging with the Psalms in this way aids in nurturing a heart filled with worship, gratitude, and reverence for God.

In essence, when one speaks to another through Psalms, it extends beyond mere words. It is an invitation to shared worship, mutual upliftment, and a profound immersion in the Word of God. Personally, the Agpeya played a pivotal role in my spiritual foundation. It is a cherished prayer book given by the church for personal devotion. Divided into seven unique hours, the Agpeya beautifully blends psalms and scriptures, drawing its essence directly from the Bible and guiding us to dedicate them in devout prayer. Engaging deeply with its passages can influence our thoughts and, in turn, our speech.

A meaningful connection was re-established with the Agpeya through an unexpected channel: a pen pal inmate, a convert with whom I exchanged letters during my church volunteering days. His deep bond with the midnight prayers was a touching testament to the profound spiritual depth the Psalms provide in reflective moments.

In the realm of the sacred, our words also bear weight. As humans, our understanding of the divine is limited, but our words can shape our relationship with the transcendent. When our language becomes disrespectful, profane, or dismissive of the sacred, we risk severing the connection we seek. Just as the Tower of Babel's builders sought to reach the heavens with arrogance, our words that offend the sacred reflect a lack of reverence and humility. The divine, which encompasses the source of meaning and purpose for many, deserves words that reflect our deep respect and appreciation for its mystery and power.

We witness the intricate impact of our words in three distinct realms—childhood, marriage, and the sacred. Just as the Tower of Babel serves as a cautionary biblical account of the consequences of hubris, our words carry the potential to either elevate or undermine, to connect or divide. Whether speaking to the vulnerable hearts of children, nurturing marital bonds, or approaching matters of the divine, the power of our words demands mindfulness, empathy, and a recognition of the profound influence they wield.

In today's ever-evolving world of communication, words have

a profound impact, and profanity is a compelling facet of this impact. The development and use of curse words are steeped in centuries of linguistic, cultural, and historical influences. The roots of many swear words can be traced back to religious contexts, where once-sacred terminologies metamorphosed over time into profane expressions. For instance, some words derived from the Latin term "damnum" have evolved from meanings like "loss" or "damage" into expressions of religious condemnation.

Furthermore, throughout history, certain words associated with bodily functions or taboo subjects have found their way into profanity. The power of these words often lies in their ability to tap into deep-rooted societal taboos, making them especially effective in conveying solid emotions or offense. Another segment of derogatory words originates from slurs aimed at specific groups based on factors like race or gender. Over time, these slurs, intended to belittle, have intensified in their offensive capacities. As language continues to evolve, so does the meaning and connotation of words. A process known as "semantic shift" can give innocuous words a newly found offensive edge, as seen with the word "bloody" in British English. However, it's paramount to remember that the impact of these words varies across cultures and societal norms. A highly offensive term in one culture may be benign in another. The ebb and flow of societal values and historical influences play a pivotal role in shaping the development and interpretation of curse words.

Research has also delved into the psychological effects of cursing. Some studies suggest that using profanity can serve as a release, providing individuals with an outlet for pent-up emotions. Such waiver may be especially crucial in moments of acute stress or pain. For instance, findings from Keele University have indicated that swearing can enhance pain tolerance, possibly triggering a "fight or flight" response. However, the relationship between swearing and stress is not universal, as individual beliefs, cultural norms, and personal reactions can vary significantly.

As we traverse the digital age, the line between genuine connection and emotional disconnection becomes increasingly blurred. The potency of words, both in healing and harming, cannot be understated. As we witness a rise in miscommunications and broken relationships, it becomes essential to understand and harness the true power of communication. By emphasizing empathy, active listening, and sincerity, we can foster genuine connections and work towards a world defined by understanding and compassion.

6

Crafting a New Discourse

Let's explore the correlation between the Tower of Babel and the advent of the internet and examine how language, communication, and human ambition intersect in both contexts. While these two concepts are separated by millennia, they reflect significant shifts in human interaction and the potential consequences of our aspirations. Just as the people of Babel used language to attempt to reach the heavens, the internet has brought about a global interconnectedness that transcends physical boundaries. The biblical story highlights the power of language to shape human endeavors and ambitions. Similarly, the internet has transformed language and communication by enabling people from diverse cultures, languages, and backgrounds to interact, share information, and collaborate on an unprecedented scale.

Both situations underscore language's potential to unite or divide, depending on how it is used. The people of Babel sought unity through a towering monument, but their arrogance led to confusion and division. In the digital age, the internet can foster unity by bringing people together, yet it can also exacerbate division through misinformation, echo chambers, and online conflicts. The ease of communication offered by the internet has the potential to connect people across the world, but it can also contribute to polarization and misunderstanding if not used responsibly. The Tower of Babel story speaks to the dangers of unchecked ambition.

The drive to achieve greatness can lead to disregarding ethical considerations. Similarly, the rapid development of the internet and digital technologies has brought tremendous advancements. Still, it also raises ethical questions about privacy, data security, online behavior, and the impact of technology on society. Just as the people of Babel faced consequences for their ambitions, our modern technological aspirations must be tempered with ethical considerations. In the Tower of Babel story, linguistic diversity was introduced to thwart the people's ambitions. On the internet, linguistic diversity persists, but technology has provided tools for translation and communication across languages. Online translation services and platforms facilitate global communication, making connecting and collaborating more accessible for people who speak different languages. This contrasts with the confusion and dispersion resulting from the incident at Babel.

The Tower of Babel and the Internet offer insights into the complexities of human communication, ambition, and the potential for unity or division. While separated by time and technological advancement, they underscore the significance of language in shaping our aspirations, the ethical considerations surrounding our ambitions, and the consequences of either coming together or drifting apart due to our efforts. The lessons from the Tower of Babel caution us to approach technological advancements, including the internet, with humility, responsibility, and an awareness of their potential impact on our interconnected world.

While the Tower of Babel story may not have directly changed the world in a tangible sense, its lasting impact lies in how it has shaped cultural, religious, and philosophical perspectives on language, ambition, unity, and division. It has contributed to human understanding and remains a timeless narrative that continues to provoke reflection and discussion.

The internet has profoundly transformed the world in various ways, touching almost every aspect of modern life. Its impact can be observed across social, economic, cultural, and technological dimensions. The internet has connected people from all corners of the world, transcending geographical boundaries. Communication, information exchange, and collaboration have become seamless across continents, allowing individuals to connect, share ideas, and engage in dialogue regardless of physical location. It serves as an expansive repository of information on virtually any topic. Online resources, educational platforms, and search engines enable individuals to access knowledge, learn new skills, and stay informed about global events. This democratization of information has empowered people to be more self-reliant learners.

Communication methods have evolved significantly with the advent of the Internet. Email, social media, video conferencing, and instant messaging have revolutionized communication, enabling real-time interactions with friends, family, colleagues, and strangers. E-commerce has flourished due to the internet, reshaping traditional business models. Online shopping, digital payments, and remote work have become integral to the global economy. The Internet has also paved the way for startups and small businesses to reach a wider audience without extensive physical infrastructure. Social media platforms have enabled people to connect, share experiences, and express opinions on a massive scale. These platforms have transformed activism, advocacy, and public discourse, allowing diverse voices to be heard.

The internet has facilitated cultural, ideas, and art exchange across borders. People can explore different cultures, languages, and traditions through online media, fostering a greater global interconnectedness. The internet has shaped political landscapes by providing platforms for political discussions, movements, and activism. Social media has allowed citizens to express their opinions, hold governments accountable, and mobilize for social change. News dissemination has shifted to online platforms, impacting traditional media outlets. While this has expanded access to news, it has also brought challenges related to misinformation, fake news, and the need for media literacy. The Internet has opened remote healthcare services (telemedicine) and online education opportunities. People can access medical consultations, courses, and learning resources from the comfort of their homes. The digital age has raised concerns about online privacy and data security. Protecting personal information and preventing cyberattacks have become essential considerations in the digital landscape. The internet has fueled innovation in technology, entertainment, and creative fields. Platforms for content creation, sharing, and collaboration have empowered individuals to showcase their talents and ideas. While it has brought immense benefits, the Internet also poses challenges that require thoughtful solutions. As the internet continues to evolve, its influence on society, culture, and daily life will remain significant, shaping the course of human progress in ways that we are only beginning to understand.

The internet has profoundly impacted younger generations, often called digital natives, who have grown up in a world where digital technologies, connectivity, and online interactions are a central part of their lives. The influence of the internet on younger generations is multifaceted and has shaped various aspects of their development, behavior, and outlook on the future. It has redefined how younger generations communicate. Social media platforms, messaging apps, and online communities have become primary avenues for connecting with friends and peers. This has facilitated global friendships and cross-cultural exchanges, but it has also raised concerns about the depth and quality of these relationships.

The Internet provides instant access to vast information and educational resources. Younger generations can learn new skills, explore diverse subjects, and pursue self-directed learning online. This could empower them with knowledge and enhance their educational experiences. It has created opportunities for younger generations to explore unconventional career paths. Freelancing, online entrepreneurship, content creation, and remote work have become viable options for earning income and pursuing passion projects. The internet has played a significant role in engaging younger generations in political discussions and social activism. Online platforms provide spaces for voicing opinions, mobilizing support for causes, and advocating for change. While the internet offers numerous benefits, it has also raised concerns about the impact on mental health. Younger generations are exposed to social comparison, cyberbullying, and excessive screen time, which can affect their psychological well-being. The digital footprint of younger generations is a growing concern. They must balance sharing personal information online and protecting their privacy. Younger generations need to develop critical thinking skills and media literacy to discern credible sources from unreliable ones. The internet allows more youthful generations to explore diverse cultures, perspectives, and identities. This exposure can lead to greater cultural awareness and empathy, but it can also lead to cultural appropriation or the spread of stereotypes.

Younger generations will continue to experience a world increasingly shaped by technology and the internet. Their ability to adapt to rapid technological changes will be crucial. The future may bring advancements in artificial intelligence, virtual reality, and other technologies that could further alter how they live, work, and interact. However, it's important to note that challenges also lie ahead. Striking a balance between online and offline life, managing screen time, maintaining genuine relationships, and addressing the potential adverse effects of technology on mental health will be ongoing concerns. The role of education in teaching responsible internet usage, critical thinking, and digital ethics will be pivotal in shaping the positive impact of the internet on younger generations. Ultimately, the future for younger generations will be defined by their ability to harness the benefits of the internet while navigating its challenges, all while contributing to shaping a digital world that is both innovative and responsible.

Is it just to completely discount the internet and technology? Certainly not. They are remarkable innovations, but they demand our responsible engagement. They should be tools of construction, not destruction. While these tools are a boon to us, in the hands of those grappling with personal challenges, be it life circumstances, mental health, or emotions, their potential can be misdirected. Yet, imagine the transformation if we inundated the digital realm with content that uplifts and inspires. Why not let positivity prevail?

7

The Profound Power
of Wyrd

An intricate thread weaves the fabric of communication, understanding, and expression in the grand arras of human existence. This thread is none other than the humble yet extraordinary entity we call "words." These seemingly simple units of language possess a profound power that transcends time, culture, and boundaries, shaping the very essence of our thoughts, emotions, and connections. Just as a skilled artist wields a brush to create captivating masterpieces or a composer orchestrates melodies to stir the soul, words are the instruments with which we compose the symphony of human experience. They hold the keys to knowledge, empathy, and the crystallization of ideas.

From ancient tales passed down through generations to the digital conversations that span the globe today, the value and significance of words stand as a testament to humanity's innate desire to share, learn, and, ultimately, connect on the deepest levels.

The word "word" itself originates from Old English "wyrd," which means "speech" or "sentence." Old English is the earliest form of English spoken and written in parts of modern-day England and southern Scotland. In the sacred journey of creation, as told in the Book of Genesis, the inception of words, like many elements of existence, originates in the divine design. When God breathed life into Adam, the first human, a cascade of understanding, expression, and connection was set into motion. Just as each word in Scripture holds layers of meaning and wisdom, so too did the first uttered words carry with them a profound significance.

In the Garden of Eden, where the splendor of nature danced in harmony, Adam and Eve began to articulate their thoughts and emotions, using language as a vessel for the exchange of ideas and feelings. Through the divine gift of speech, humanity was given the power to name the earth's creatures, commune with the Creator, and impart knowledge to one another. The journey of words throughout biblical history parallels the evolution of humanity's relationship with God and one another. From the sacred texts that guide and inspire to the parables that illustrate deeper truths, words serve as bridges between the temporal and the eternal. In the stories of prophets, psalmists, and disciples, words become instruments of revelation, compassion, and transformation. Just as God's Word is said to have spoken the universe into existence, the words we use hold the potential to shape reality, heal wounds, and forge connections. From the tower of Babel to the tongues of Pentecost, the Bible reflects the complexities of language and its power to divide and unite. Thus, the significance of words, from their divine inception to their earthly application, is woven intricately into the narrative of faith, guiding us to communicate with reverence, empathy, and purpose.

The Bible's story provides profound insights into the complexities of language and its dual nature to unite and divide humanity. In the Book of Genesis, the story portrays a moment of linguistic division. As the descendants of Noah gathered to build a tower that would reach the heavens, they sought to make a name for themselves. However, God confounded their language in response to their pride, causing them to speak in different tongues. This linguistic confusion led to the dispersion of people across the Earth, as they could not understand each other. This story illustrates the power of language to create barriers and divisions among humans. The diverse languages that emerged from this event fragmented humanity into separate groups, inhibiting effective communication and collaboration. The narrative serves as a cautionary story, highlighting the consequences of arrogance and the misuse of language. It offers insights into why this event occurred and what lessons can be gleaned from it.

The power of words cannot be overstated. They are the primary tools we use to express our thoughts, feelings, and intentions. Through words, we convey love, anger, joy, sorrow, and every emotion in between. However, just as they have the power to uplift and heal, they also have the potential to wound deeply. It's essential, therefore, to recognize the lessons we can learn from misusing them.

When we misuse words, especially in our interactions with others, we inadvertently reveal our insecurities, biases, or unresolved issues. For instance, people might lash out in anger or frustration, using sharper and more hurtful words than intended. This usually reflects more about the speaker's emotional state than the person they're speaking to. Harsh words can create rifts that are hard to mend. A single derogatory comment can erode trust that took years to build. It's a sobering thought that moments of careless speech can result in lasting divisions between friends, family, and communities. Such divides can be seen in personal relationships and on a larger scale in society, where rhetoric can unite or polarize groups.

Another consequence of misusing words is the effect on the individual at the receiving end. When people are constantly belittled or criticized, their self-worth is challenged. They begin to doubt their abilities and, over time, might internalize the negativity, leading to a decrease in self-esteem. This demotivation can manifest in various ways: decreased productivity, loss of passion, or even withdrawal from social interactions. On the other hand, words can be tools of empowerment. Positive affirmations, encouragement, and genuine compliments can spur individuals to reach greater heights. By being more deliberate in our words, we can foster environments where individuals feel valued, understood, and motivated. As we navigate personal relationships and societal interactions, we must be mindful of our words' weight. The lessons learned from misusing words are about avoiding negative impacts and recognizing the incredible potential words must shape lives and societies for the better.

Misusing words when speaking to ourselves can profoundly affect our psyche and overall well-being. In essence, we become both the speaker and the listener of our internal dialogue, amplifying the effects of every word, whether positive or negative. When this dialogue is riddled with negativity, it molds our perceptions and attitudes, often more than we might initially realize. When individuals continually berate or belittle themselves internally, it often fosters a damaging self-image. Such thoughts like "I'm not good enough," "I always mess things up," or "No one would ever care about me" can take root sincerely, becoming core beliefs that dictate how we approach the world. Over time, these harmful words can manifest into self-limiting behaviors and feelings of worthlessness.

Moreover, consistently misusing words in our internal narrative can affect our mental health. It can lead to heightened levels of anxiety, depression, and stress. For instance, an individual might catastrophize situations, always assuming the worst outcome, or overly criticize themselves for minor mistakes, never allowing for self-forgiveness. However, it's crucial to recognize that this internal dialogue, while potent, is malleable. Just as we can harm ourselves with negative words, we equally possess the ability to heal and empower. The practice of positive self-affirmation, where one consciously reinforces positive beliefs and attitudes about oneself, can act as an antidote. Over time, replacing the negative internal narrative with one of kindness, understanding, and love can radically transform one's self-perception and life trajectory. While misusing words in our internal dialogue can have damaging consequences, awareness of this narrative and intentional efforts to shift it can pave the way for self-acceptance, growth, and mental well-being.

The phenomenon of humans leaning toward negative speech patterns, commonly termed the "negativity bias," is deeply rooted in our psychology and history. Historically, from an evolutionary perspective, this bias towards the negative might have conferred survival benefits. Our ancestors were surrounded by constant threats, ranging from wild predators to hostile tribes. Thus, being especially alert to potential dangers and retaining memories of adverse outcomes was crucial. In essence, focusing on the negative was a mechanism to ensure survival. Moreover, our cognitive structure seems to assign more weight to adverse events than positive ones. A single criticism or negative encounter can overshadow numerous compliments or positive interactions. This heightened emotional response to adverse events ensures that they remain etched in our memory, making us more inclined to ruminate on them and subsequently communicate these sentiments.

Adding complexity to this predisposition is the socio-cultural environment we're immersed in. Today's society, with its rampant competition, emphasis on perfectionism, and the ubiquity of comparison, especially in the digital age of social media, can exacerbate feelings of inadequacy. When individuals are continually subjected to these pressures, their internal dialogue can become increasingly hostile, influencing their external communication. Furthermore, contemporary media, with its propensity for sensationalism, tends to highlight negative news, perpetuating a worldview that emphasizes negativity. Another crucial factor is the reinforcement loops created by consistent negative feedback. If pessimistic peers frequently surround an individual or persistently receive negative feedback, it reinforces their negative speech patterns. This cycle can be self-perpetuating, leading to entrenched negative communication habits.

The people's misguided pursuit of agreement in the Book of Genesis without proper reverence for God's authority led to division. The confusion of languages disrupted their unity, scattering them across the Earth and isolating them from one another due to their inability to communicate effectively. God intervened by confounding their speech in response to their pride and defiance. This intervention was not a punishment out of cruelty but rather an act of mercy and correction. By dispersing the people and confusing their language, God curtailed their misguided ambitions and reminded them of their dependence on Him. This divine intervention was intended to prevent further harm from their arrogant pursuits. The Tower of Babel story ultimately teaches us the importance of humility, proper stewardship of the gift of words we have been given, and the necessity of aligning our ambitions with God's will. It warns against the dangers of using language and abilities for self-glorification rather than for the betterment of humanity and fulfilling God's purposes. The consequences of this story remind us that true unity and understanding arise from humility, cooperation, and the acknowledgment of our place in the grand design of creation.

Though we have history as our guide and contemporary challenges as catalysts for growth, we often find ourselves entangled in repetitive cycles. The underlying reason for this persistent pattern is multifaceted. Human nature resists change at the core, often favoring the familiar over the uncharted. This preference for the known, even if detrimental, can be more comfortable than embracing the uncertainties of change. Moreover, societal structures and deeply ingrained beliefs can further reinforce these cycles, making it challenging to break free. It is also worth noting that the collective memory tends to be short-lived, leading to the repetition of past mistakes. Until we confront these intrinsic and extrinsic barriers head-on, genuine progression remains elusive.

Our tendency to veer toward harmful speech is not merely a byproduct of evolutionary mechanisms, cognitive biases, socio-cultural pressures, or the feedback loops we find ourselves trapped in. While recognizing these factors is essential, the first step towards cultivating healthier communication patterns, we must address an even deeper underlying cause. This root issue lies in our disconnection from the very source of words, their meaning, and vitality. When we drift away from Christ, the One who gave words their profound essence, we inadvertently misguide our verbal expressions. This spiritual disconnect influences our language and profoundly impacts our minds and hearts, emphasizing the importance of grounding ourselves in faith.

8

Unveiling Parallels

What do my words, the Tower of Babel and the Internet, have in common?

The concept of words as lethal weapons parallels the story of the Tower of Babel and our modern internet age. In the Tower of Babel story, where human ambition leads to confusion and division through misused communication, my words wielded negatively can inflict emotional, psychological, or physical harm. Like the Tower of Babel, the internet symbolizes our collective aspiration for global connectivity, yet it carries the potential for misuse. While the internet was designed to foster knowledge sharing and unity, its misuse through spreading misinformation, hate, and privacy invasion reflects a deviation from its positive intent. This cycle echoes the human tendency to misuse what's intended for good, prompting us to reflect on our ethical responsibility. In both cases, be it the Tower of Babel or the Internet, the lessons underscore the need for humility, ethical considerations, and mindful use of powerful tools to ensure our actions align with the original intentions for good.

In the realm of profound questions, a beacon of truth emerges: What is the essence of the good word, or could it be that the question transformed should be: Who embodies the ultimate expression of the good Word? This brings us to the concept of the "Logos," often referred to as the living Word. In philosophical and theological contexts, the Logos represents the divine reason or creative principle that gives order to the universe. This rich concept has deep roots, drawing connections across cultures and beliefs.

At the heart of this contemplation lies the notion of the Word that is communicated and alive, resonating through time and dimensions. Logos transcends linguistic confines, encompassing meanings beyond mere definitions. Much like the Tower of Babel, which signified humanity's ambition to touch the divine, the Logos embodies the aspiration to comprehend the ineffable, to articulate the unspoken, and to fathom the unfathomable. Drawing from various spiritual traditions, the Logos finds resonance as the divine source of wisdom and the conduit through which existence was brought into being. It bridges the gap between the finite and the infinite.

Who embodies the living Word? As we delve into the heart of the Logos and the living Word, we embark on a journey that transcends the limitations of language, revealing a truth that unites the ancient and the contemporary, the sacred and the secular. The quest to understand the essence of the good Word and its embodiment in the living Logos beckons us to ponder the interconnectedness of all things and the potential for transformation through the power of words and ideas.

"In the beginning was the Word, and the Word was with God, and the Word was God." John 1:1

Diving into Christian theology, especially as depicted in the Gospel of John, "Logos" denotes the role of Jesus Christ. John's Gospel begins with the profound statement, "In the beginning was the Word [Logos], and the Word [Logos] was with God, and the Word [Logos] was God," underscoring the divine wisdom and the eternal principle through which everything was created and sustained. "Logos" translates to "word" or "speech" in Greek, typically referring to either spoken or written discourse.

This verse is a powerful and profound statement about the nature of the divine Word (Logos) and its relationship to God. It's often interpreted as highlighting the eternal existence of the Word, its religious character, and its close connection to God. These opening words from the Gospel of John resonate through the annals of time, encapsulating a profound truth that echoes across belief systems and philosophies. This ancient proclamation delves into the heart of creation, encapsulating the concept of the Logos, the divine principle that infuses meaning, purpose, and order into the cosmos. These words transcend mere language; they unveil a cosmic symphony where the Word emerges as the agent of creation and the divine mediator between the finite and the infinite. The connection between the Logos and the Creator is unbreakable—a relationship woven into the fabric of existence. This enigmatic verse, akin to the Tower of Babel's reaching for the heavens, calls upon humanity to seek understanding and connection with the divine through the Word.

"In the beginning was the Word," a timeless proclamation that spans cultures and faiths, resonates through the ages, guiding seekers to understand that the Word—the Logos—is not only a divine utterance but a living, transformative force. It beckons us to recognize the sacredness of communication, the potential of words to shape realities, and the responsibility we bear as custodians of this power. As we ponder the relationship between the divine Word and the human experience, we are reminded that our words, like the Tower's builders, reach for the religious, and it is our choice whether they carry arrogance or humility, division or unity, harm, or healing.

The Logos, intimately connected to God yet distinct, is portrayed as both the agent of creation and the embodiment of divine wisdom. Delving deeper, this declaration has profound implications for human experience. As we ponder the interplay between the Holy Word and our lives, parallels with the Tower of Babel story come into focus. Just as the Tower's builders aspired to reach the heavenly heights, our words also possess the power to go for the divine, shaping our reality. Like the builders' ambitious tower, our words serve as conduits for our intentions and aspirations. They can be instruments of enlightenment, manipulation tools, bridges of connection, or walls of division. The power vested in our words is akin to the divine creative power that shaped the universe. Our choice is whether our words carry the weight of arrogance, attempting to usurp the religious order, or the humility to recognize our place within it.

The Tower of Babel narrative cautions against the perils

of unchecked ambition and the consequences of misusing communication. Similarly, the internet can mirror Tower's initiatives as we navigate the digital age. It offers unprecedented connectivity and a platform for exchanging ideas, yet its potential for division and harm remains evident. Just as language confusion scattered the builders, misinformation, and discord can fragment our modern global community. In contrast, we harness the potential for unity and healing if we wield our words with mindfulness, compassion, and empathy.

The Gospel's assertion that "the Word was God" reminds us that our comments reflect our inner state, capable of carrying or distorting the divine presence. They can offer solace, promote understanding, and foster harmony, healing the divisions that plague humanity. As we contemplate the relationship between the holy Word and human experience, we find ourselves at the crossroads of profound responsibility. Our words can further fragment a world seeking connection or contribute to its restoration. Choosing words that resonate with divine harmony is within our reach, echoing the Logos' eternal wisdom. Just as the Tower's builders sought to bridge the earthly and the heavenly, our words can bridge hearts, cultures, and nations, fostering unity and healing in a world yearning for both.

When the Word is described as a "double-edged sword," its dual nature comes to light—both a source of profound positive impact and potential harm. Like a sharp blade, the Word can illuminate truths, guide paths, and offer protection, yet it can also cut through misunderstandings, perpetuate divisions, and cause conflict. These dual aspects remind us of the profound responsibility we bear in our communication, urging us to wield the Word and all our words with mindfulness, wisdom, and an awareness of the far-reaching consequences they can carry.

The concept of the Word bringing life and conviction is deeply intertwined with spiritual and religious contexts, symbolizing the transformative power of divine teachings and truths. The idea that the Word brings life suggests its capacity to infuse existence with meaning, purpose, and vitality, offering guidance on ethical conduct. Simultaneously, the Word's ability to convict involves shedding light on the truth, leading to introspection and personal transformation. This conviction process arises from recognizing one's imperfections and prompts a desire for self-improvement and a closer relationship with the divine and others. Together, these aspects underscore the profound impact of the Holy Word, which, when embraced, not only imparts meaning to life but also guides individuals on a journey of self-discovery, growth, and alignment with higher principles.

The divine power's ability to overcome us is often explored within spiritual and religious traditions, reflecting the transformative and transcendent nature of the Holy. The overcoming of individuals by divine power is a testament to the profound and often ineffable influence of the sacred within human lives. This experience transcends the boundaries of ordinary existence, evoking a sense of awe and humility in the face of something greater than us. The divine power's ability to overcome us can manifest in various ways—through moments of profound insight, spiritual awakening, or a deep inner knowing that goes beyond rational comprehension.

At times, this overcoming might be gentle, a gradual realization that draws us closer to a higher truth and purpose. Other times, it can be a powerful, overwhelming encounter that transforms our perspective, beliefs, and identity. In these instances, the divine power becomes a force that breaks down barriers, dissolves ego-driven limitations, and opens us to a deeper connection with the sacred. It can lead to a profound sense of peace, joy, and alignment with God's divine order. This overcoming is not about domination or control but rather an invitation to surrender to the divine flow and wisdom. It's an acknowledgment that human experience is part of a more excellent plan, and the divine power guides us toward growth, understanding, and a more profound relationship with the sacred.

However, this experience is deeply personal and can vary significantly among individuals. Some may encounter divine power through contemplative practices, prayer, or moments of deep introspection. Others might experience it in the beauty of nature, the kindness of others, or moments of uncertainty that feel divinely orchestrated. Ultimately, the overcoming by divine power reflects the mystery and awe of the spiritual journey. It's an ongoing alignment, transformation, and connection with something beyond our understanding—an experience that can reshape our lives, perspectives, and relationships with the world around us.

9

The Liturgy of the Word

The word "liturgical" pertains to liturgy or public worship. It is most often used in the context of religious ceremonies or rituals, especially in Christian traditions. Specifically, it relates to the order and form of services and rites. The liturgy became my sanctuary when reading the Bible or praying seemed beyond my reach. I would find myself seated quietly in a pew in church, merely listening without actively participating. However, the mere act of being in such a sacred space brought tranquility to my restless spirit. While the church's primary purpose is to foster fellowship among believers, I needed isolation. The gentle, unspoken prayers and the whispers of faith resonated within me, providing the solace my soul desperately craved.

The liturgical hymns also played a pivotal role in my

spiritual journey. Their resonance, rooted in hymnology, offered an experience akin to meditation, guiding the soul into deep reflection and connection. Coupled with this was the aroma of the incense, which awakened my senses and created an ethereal atmosphere. It felt like I was being gently ushered into a paradisiacal realm, transcending the mundane and connecting with God. The liturgy stands as a profound three-hour service, marked by the priest's fervent prayers, the melodic chants of the deacons, and the responsive echoes of the congregation. Within this sacred time, idle chatter finds no place; a deep sense of devotion consumes the entire atmosphere. There's an undeniable upliftment in being enveloped by fellow worshippers. Their reverence for God, respect for the sanctuary, and their palpable awareness of the divine presence are constant reminders of the holiness surrounding us all. It's more than just a service; it's a communal journey towards the sacred.

Raised within the embrace of the Coptic Church, I was enveloped by the resonant verses of St. Basil's Liturgy every week and the memorable cadences of St. Gregory's during the feasts. For years, these words felt like mere background noise, echoing weekly as I stood somewhat detached in the congregation. This ritual continued unbroken for nearly two decades. Then, life's unpredictable tide pulled me, reducing my presence in the church to just the liturgy's tail end. Yet, the little girl who once passively stood in church has transformed. Once seemingly dormant, those words had sown seeds in me and blossomed over time.

The Liturgy of the Word in the Coptic Church, also called the "Liturgy of the Catechumens," is the initial segment of the Divine Liturgy, preceding the Liturgy of the Faithful. Rooted in ancient Christian practices, it centers around the proclamation and teaching of the Word of God. The ceremony commences with reading the Pauline Epistle, typically an excerpt from one of St. Paul's letters. The Catholic Epistle, a reading from the general epistles of other apostles such as St. James or St. Peter, follows this. Subsequently, a passage from the Acts of the Apostles, which details the early Christian Church's history and the apostles' journeys, is recited. The highlight of this segment is the reading from the Holy Gospel, where a particular event or teaching from the life of Jesus Christ is narrated. These readings include hymns, responses, and doxologies that celebrate the mysteries of the Christian faith. For instance, before the Gospel reading, the congregation sings the "Alleluia," a joyful exclamation, signaling reverence and anticipation for the words of Christ about to be proclaimed. The Liturgy of the Word is not just a passive hearing of scriptures. Still, it is considered an active encounter with God's living Word, fostering spiritual growth and deepening the understanding of the faith among the congregation.

Central to many liturgical traditions is the emphasis on sacraments, particularly the Eucharist, which serve as profound, tangible connections between the believer and the divine realm. The structured nature of liturgy provides predictable touchpoints for spiritual reflection, with its scriptural foundation and theological depth allowing for deep engagement with the faith. Amidst the ebb and flow of life, the consistency of liturgical worship offers an emotional anchor, a sanctuary of stability and transcendence in an ever-evolving world.

The Holy Spirit's presence during the liturgy is foundational, serving as the living breath that animates the words and rituals, transforming them from mere formality into vibrant experiences of the Divine. Every chant, prayer, and gesture is imbued with intention in the liturgy. While the words and rituals have profound significance, the Holy Spirit brings them to life, making them resonant and transformative. Just as the early disciples were imbued with the Spirit at Pentecost and spoke in tongues that touched the hearts of diverse listeners, the liturgy, through the Holy Spirit, speaks a language that transcends human understanding and touches the soul.

The role of the Holy Spirit in liturgy can be likened to the breath that gives life to the body. Words, without the Spirit, can risk becoming hollow or rote, but when animated by the Spirit, they come alive, piercing hearts and drawing believers deeper into communion with God. The sacraments, especially the Eucharist, are moments where this is most palpable. Through the work of the Holy Spirit, the bread and wine become, for believers, the Body, and Blood of Christ. It's a mystery that defies logical understanding but is central to the faith experience of millions.

For those who question the enigma of the Eucharist, consider this: How is it that two individuals enter a church and emerge united in holy matrimony? Marriage is more than a social or legal agreement; it's a sacred covenant made in the presence of God. As couples stand at the altar, they engage in profound acts that symbolize their union. They exchange solemn vows, promising before God to love, honor, and cherish one another, emphasizing the divine nature of their commitment. The exchange of rings, symbols of unbroken eternity, further reinforces this commitment as a tangible reminder of their pledge to each other. The priest oversees these promises and invokes God's blessings on the couple, praying for their journey ahead. In essence, while two individuals walk into the church, God's hand is believed to unite them as one during the sacred ceremony. As experienced in sacraments such as communion, marriage, baptism, and confession, the Spirit of God is a profound mystery. "Mystery" refers to something beyond human comprehension or understanding. This enigma eludes a clear definition or explanation. In religious and theological contexts, a mystery often denotes a divine truth or reality that, while partially revealed, remains incomprehensible to the human mind. It's a truth that can be experienced or believed in but never fully grasped or delineated.

It's remarkable how human nature often gravitates towards believing the vast and sometimes unfounded narratives presented by the world, accepting them without much scrutiny. Yet, many wrestle with doubt and skepticism regarding God's divine truths and promises. The irony is palpable. We quickly welcome what is fleeting and transient but question the eternal and unwavering. Perhaps the vastness and depth of God's truths make them challenging to grasp fully. They are profound and transcendent, often eluding our limited human comprehension. Yet, this very nature of God makes faith a vital aspect of belief. Ultimately, it's a journey of trust, where we recognize that we may never understand everything, but we can still believe in its truth and authenticity.

Furthermore, the Holy Spirit acts as a guide and comforter during the liturgy, interceding and praying on behalf of believers, even when they may not have the words themselves. The Apostle Paul writes in Romans 8:26, "The Spirit helps us in our weakness. We do not know what to pray for as we ought, but the Spirit intercedes for us with groanings too deep for words." The Holy Spirit is the dynamic force during the liturgy. It takes ancient words and rituals and makes them relevant, alive, and potent for each believer in every context and across time. It bridges the gap between the heavenly and the earthly, making the liturgy a living encounter with the Divine.

Rather than being a mere rote exercise, repetition in liturgy acts as a spiritual anchor, grounding and shaping the believer's faith journey. This rhythmic constancy, reminiscent of a heartbeat pulsing life through a body, embeds sacred truths deep within the soul. Over time, repeated prayers and chants become woven into the fabric of a worshipper's consciousness, shaping their worldview and spiritual reflexes. Among these repeated elements, phrases like "Lord, have mercy" and the Lord's Prayer hold particular significance. The plea for mercy is a humbling reminder of human frailty and God's boundless grace, guiding believers toward repentance and gratitude. On the other hand, the Lord's Prayer, given by Christ Himself, encapsulates the essence of Christian faith and hope. Its repetition serves as a communal affirmation of trust in God's providence, kingdom, and will. Through these recitations, worshippers are continually reminded of their relationship with the Divine, reinforcing their commitment and understanding of sacred truths.

Repetition carries a profound weight across diverse cultures and religions, symbolizing perfection. I frequently find myself reiterating things thrice, and similarly, I need to hear others say something three times for clarity. The need for individuals to listen to things three times can be rooted in several cognitive and psychological factors. Repetition plays a vital role in strengthening memory retention. By hearing information multiple times, the brain reinforces the neural pathways associated with it, making it easier to recall later. Additionally, in our modern era, rife with distractions, a person's attention can waver. A singular presentation of information might be missed due to a fleeting distraction or lapse in concentration. Reiterations ensure that even if someone's focus drifts the first time, they have subsequent opportunities to grasp the message. Furthermore, some information demands a degree of cognitive processing, and repeated exposure provides the brain ample time to assimilate and understand the content.

I was captivated by Jesus posing the same question to Peter thrice. The moment where Jesus asks Peter the same question three times is profoundly symbolic and significant in the New Testament. Found in John 21:15-17, after His resurrection, Jesus repeatedly asks Peter if he loves Him, to which Peter responds affirmatively each time. This tri-fold questioning can be viewed as a redemptive act for Peter, who, before Jesus's crucifixion, had denied knowing Jesus three times. By asking Peter three times if he loves Him, Jesus offers Peter a chance at reconciliation and restoration. The repeated questioning underscores Peter's commitment to Jesus and emphasizes their relationship's profound nature of forgiveness and renewal. It is a poignant reminder of Jesus's boundless mercy and the transformative power of genuine repentance and love.

The inclination for me to repeat things thrice, or the need to hear them three times, can be rooted in various reasons, both spiritual and cognitive. Drawing parallels with Peter's redemption might indicate a subconscious desire for affirmation or understanding, echoing deeper spiritual or emotional themes in one's life. On the other hand, it also hints at cognitive patterns or an undiagnosed learning challenge that benefits from repetition to solidify comprehension. Humans often seek ways in behavior and cognition to make sense of the world and their place in it.

Number three holds a special reverence in many cultural and religious contexts. For instance, in Christianity, the Holy Trinity—Father, Son, and Holy Spirit—anchors the faith, making the number three emblematic of divine completeness. Beyond symbolic resonance, triadic repetition also has practical implications. Reiterating something thrice ensures emphasis, aids memorization, and underscores its importance. It's a pattern that the human psyche finds compelling, facilitating more profound understanding and resonance. Whether seen in literary devices, such as the "rule of three" in storytelling or sacred rituals and prayers, this repetition underscores the universal and enduring power of the triad in conveying emphasis and significance. What I initially dismissed as redundant and monotonous became a personal ritual, compelling me to echo everything thrice. Yet, even more captivating is my newfound attraction to repetitive liturgical worship and how, within its structure, the words pulsate with life.

10

From Weapons to Wisdom

We live in a world inundated with words. From fleeting text messages to age-old literature, from passionate speeches to casual conversations, words envelop our existence. Yet, amid this constant barrage, some words stand out, taking root in our hearts and leaving an indelible mark. These are the words spoken in the love language of "Words of Affirmation."

Understanding Words of Affirmation as a Love Language

At its core, words of affirmation refer to any spoken or written affirmation that acknowledges and appreciates another's qualities or actions. For those who identify with this love language, these words aren't just casual compliments but lifelines. They are the assurance of being seen, valued, and cherished.

In his groundbreaking work "The Five Love Languages," Dr. Gary Chapman introduced words of affirmation as one of the primary ways individuals feel loved and valued. When these individuals hear phrases like "I'm proud of you," "You mean so much to me," or "You did a great job," they don't just register them as niceties; they absorb them as genuine validations of their worth.

But why do words hold such a potent impact? Several reasons underpin this phenomenon:

1. From early childhood, words have been our primary tool for understanding our environment. Parents' affirmations or criticisms shape our self-worth, confidence, and view of the world. When someone with the love language of words of affirmation receives positive reinforcement, it can heal old wounds and create new, positive associations.

2. Words, incredibly when genuine, act as a mirror, reflecting aspects of ourselves we might overlook. When someone notices and articulates our efforts or qualities, these facets become clearer, reinforcing our identity.

3. Every person battles internal critics. For those whose primary love language is words of affirmation, external validation can be a powerful antidote to self-doubt and negative self-perception.

The Weight of Words on My Heart

For me, words are more than mere sounds; they are anchors. They anchor my self-worth, perception of my place in the world, and connections with others. Positive affirmations don't just make me happy; they fortify my spirit, equip me to face challenges, and remind me of my inherent worth.

However, with such sensitivity to words comes vulnerability. Negative remarks, even when unintentional, can pierce deeper than expected. But over time, I've come to appreciate this sensitivity. It makes me more empathetic, attentive to the words I use, and deeply grateful for the affirmations I receive.

In a world transformed by the consistent positivity of our words and those of others, the repercussions would touch every facet of our existence. First and foremost, relationships would undergo a metamorphosis. As words nurture and affirm, the bonds between friends, families, and marriages deepen, becoming bastions of trust and emotional connectivity. This shift would also significantly bolster mental well-being. Positive affirmations would elevate collective self-worth and confidence by counteracting the internal negative narratives many grapple with. Moreover, such an atmosphere would transcend personal spaces, permeating schools, and workplaces. Productivity would likely surge as collaborative environments thrive on mutual respect and understanding. Additionally, conflicts born from misunderstandings or hasty negative words would be reduced, leading to more harmonious communities. In this envisioned world, every encouraging word acts as a brick, building a society characterized by empathy, mutual support, and holistic growth.

If the current generation were to embrace the consistent positivity of words wholly, future generations would inherit a profoundly changed world. Children would be raised on a foundation of security and affirmation, leading to higher self-esteem and confidence during their formative years. This environment would naturally cultivate enhanced emotional intelligence, with younger generations becoming adept at understanding, expressing, and managing emotions constructively. These skills would translate to stronger interpersonal relationships, fewer conflicts, and a more profound sense of empathy. Moreover, with the previous generations paving the way, societal norms would shift towards collaboration and mutual respect, reducing the barriers of prejudice, discrimination, and misunderstanding. Ultimately, by instilling the power of positive communication today, we would be gifting future generations a world where emotional and mental well-being takes center stage, creating a society equipped for united growth and shared prosperity.

11

Transforming Dialog

God's Word has a unique origin, purpose, and impact.

God's Word is eternal, unchanging, and absolute. It presents spiritual, moral, and ethical directives, positioning itself as a wellspring of wisdom, truth, and everlasting promises. It imparts guidance and lays down a foundational framework for life. It molds individual beliefs, values, and actions and has a pervasive influence on communities, cultures, and civilizations, leaving an indelible mark over the ages.

God's Word is a force of power that performs miracles that defy natural logic. This belief is deeply rooted in the many accounts from the New Testament. In the book of Luke, there's a recounting of the Miraculous Catch of Fish. After a fruitless night of fishing, Jesus instructed Simon Peter to cast his net into the deep. Skeptical but obedient, Peter was astonished to haul in a net overflowing with fish, so much so that it began to tear. Another poignant example is from the Gospel of Mark, where a paralyzed man, lowered through a roof into Jesus's presence, was forgiven of his sins and healed instantaneously. Jesus said, "Get up, take your mat, and go home," showcasing the transformative power of God's Word. Yet, perhaps one of the most dramatic miracles is the Raising of Lazarus, as detailed in the Gospel of John. Lazarus had been dead for four days, yet with Jesus's proclamation, he was brought back to life. These miracles, among numerous others, underscore the profound belief in the power and potency of God's Word.

Does simply reading scripture guarantee a harmonious life? Will challenges cease to exist? Does it imply you'll attain perfection and immunity from life's struggles? Far from being a magical elixir that promises instant transformation, the Bible is a beacon, casting light on the many complexities of existence. Take a moment to contemplate your life—the relationships you cherish, the individuals you interact with daily, and the principles you are guided by.

Throughout the Bible, God provides guidance, sets directives, and lays the foundation for righteous living. Yet, time and again, humans question His authority.

The inevitable question arises: Why do we resist?

At the core of our resistance lies an inherent need for autonomy, a reluctance to surrender control to a force greater than ourselves. We crave recognition, a validation of our existence through the eyes and ears of others. This deep-seated desire to be known, to be seen, and to influence our destinies often overshadows the presence of a Higher Power. In our pursuit of self-affirmation, the Creator, the guiding force that offers a path of deeper understanding and connection, sometimes becomes a faint echo in the background of our lives. We find the true battleground of faith at this juncture of spiritual tension. To relinquish control is to embrace vulnerability, to trust in a plan grander than one we could envisage for ourselves.

Yet, in surrendering, we do not lose ourselves; instead, we open the possibility to forge a more prosperous, more nuanced relationship with the divine and, consequently, with the world around us. We are invited to explore this delicate steadiness between self-assertion and surrender, between the ego's desires and the soul's yearnings. It is a journey of deep reflection, of learning to navigate the narrow pathway that balances human will with divine guidance. Join me as we venture further, daring to question, to seek, and to find the harmony that exists when we allow ourselves to be both the conductor and the conducted, moving in synergy with a Higher Power that seeks not to overshadow but to elevate, not to silence but to harmonize, fostering a richer, deeper, and more authentic expression of our true selves.

Why do we meticulously adhere to societal norms and rules yet grapple with living by the tenets of God's Word? Why does the simple transition of a traffic light from red to green compel our obedience so effortlessly? What indeed commands our reverence? Is it the fear of a crash or the dread of being penalized? Consider the punctuality we maintain for our jobs. Is it the ticking clock or the potential repercussions of tardiness that keep us punctual? And when we grace the premises of an upscale restaurant, why do we willingly conform to their dress code? At themed celebrations, what prompts us to embrace the occasion's attire? Indeed, our daily lives are riddled with instances that reflect our underlying motivations. Yet, there appears to be a dissonance regarding matters of faith. We place blind faith in a physician we've just met or trust an attorney about whom we know little. We consume medications, believing in their curative properties, and often, we're willing to entrust our very lives to friends.

Have you noticed that when a song resonates with you, you find yourself humming its lyrics? Hearing, significantly when repeated or emotionally charged, profoundly influences the mind. When we encounter auditory stimuli, it can lead to memory formation and recall. For instance, songs from our past can swiftly take us back to a specific moment or feeling. This is why auditory mnemonics are frequently employed in education, harnessing the power of sound to aid memory. Music has a unique ability to resonate emotionally with us. A specific track or tone can induce joy and nostalgia to sadness and motivation. Advertisers and filmmakers capitalize on this emotional impact of sound, selecting clear soundtracks to elicit emotions from their audiences. Additionally, hearing remains a primary channel for learning, influencing our cognitive development from a young age. Or when you come across a humorous jest, you're eager to share it? And those catchy phrases? They often roll off your tongue effortlessly, don't they?

Such reflections prompt a deeper introspection about the nature of our trust and belief systems. What influences our choices, and how do we reconcile these with our spiritual convictions? God consistently honors every word He utters and upholds every promise He makes. Yet, our challenge often lies in reconciling that His methods and timings seldom align with our own. As a result, we tend to overlook Him, sometimes even resorting to indifference, negligence, or ridicule. In doing so, we inadvertently diminish the significance and value of His ways and words.

At the heart of our challenges is often a failure to acknowledge our constraints. When faced with hardships, our instinctive reaction is to ascribe it to divine retribution, directing blame at God rather than confronting human imperfections. Yet, God is not the embodiment of wickedness; His teachings are rooted in kindness and enlightenment. Rather than imposing His fury on His progeny, God bestows us to walk the path of virtue and avoid hostility. Visualize being trapped in a scorching, forsaken space, consumed by impenetrable shadows and encircled by animosity. Such profound desolation is a harrowing notion. It represents the abyss of life without God, devoid of His illuminating presence, guiding words, and unwavering direction.

12

Transforming Destiny

Our contention with the Word of God, or God Himself, arises from our tendency to limit Him within our narrow frameworks. We often perceive Him as a strict enforcer, demanding adherence to His rules—either His way or no way at all. What we overlook is that His Word illuminates the path to enlightenment. It serves as the conduit to love, peace, and joy, offering the key to freedom from the self-imposed shackles that bind us.

Have you ever paused to ponder the origin of your beliefs or ideas? Perhaps they took root during your childhood church visits with family or stem from judgments passed by religious figures. However, remember that figures of religious authority, those representing God, are mere mortals—flawed and striving to enact God's will as best they can. They don't possess all answers nor discern the depths of your heart or thoughts. What resonates with them might not align with you. If we delve into the scriptures, it's evident that God interacts uniquely with every individual. His boundless love extends to everyone, yet its manifestation varies. As Jesus advised Peter concerning John the Beloved — to essentially focus on his journey — we too should refrain from judging God's unique relationship with each of us. If we genuinely seek the essence of His teachings, it can be encapsulated in a singular, powerful word: Love. To grasp the depth of this divine affection, immerse yourself in 1 Corinthians 13.

Reflecting on my childhood, I remember my father reading Bible stories to my siblings and me. At the time, they felt like mere tales. Yet, my father was sowing seeds of wisdom deep within our minds. Those words have since taken root, becoming an indelible part of me. They remained present even if I only sometimes adhered to or fully comprehended them. Every moment spent in that ritual was invaluable. Reading the Bible is foundational, enriching our knowledge. Even if we don't initially accept its teachings, our minds retain them. However, what truly animated those scriptures was witnessing my father embodying them in his daily life. This distinction is vital. While it's essential to approach the Word of God with reverence and respect, it's the act of living out its teachings that truly breathes life into them.

I intend to pen this book not to lead you astray or suggest you emulate my ways. Like many, I am not immune to imperfections; my thoughts and actions can be marred with ill intentions. Sometimes, I am swayed by emotions, neglecting the truth, or I choose to accept falsehoods over reality. While working on this book, I grappled with trusting God over the words of cherished and respected individuals. It was challenging to discern that some of their advice stemmed from their pain rather than the truth. This journey taught me the importance of silencing external voices to listen to God honestly.

But how does one "hear" God? Is it an audible voice or a face-to-face conversation? For me, it's a deep spiritual connection. I perceive, absorb, and interpret His teachings via His Word. Despite the challenges I faced, I was confronted with choices. Which words should I place my faith in? Whose voice should I heed? Is the Word of God potent enough to triumph? Interestingly, I encountered similar dilemmas when composing my inaugural book, but my approach differed. Since 2017, I've realized the importance of immersing fully in God's Word for direction. I've learned to confide judiciously in trusted allies and to solicit prayers without divulging all details, for God knows every nuance. Time has shown me that God communicates in myriad ways.

I am not merely putting words on paper but simultaneously navigating a challenging life lesson. For years, I wrestled with a difficult situation, armed with words that were more like weapons. I even sported God's Word, not as it was meant to be - a source of solace and guidance - but in a way that mirrored my internal battles. I manipulated its sanctity to suit my narrative. However, in this tumultuous journey, a transformative moment arrived. It enveloped me in a profound silence, a quiet time where words, once my fiercest allies, vanished. This silence, devoid of the clamor of fighting words, became a realm of introspection and growth. I began to discern the distinction between mere words, ones borne out of pain and ego, and the true essence of God's Word, rooted in love, peace, and understanding. It was a moment of reckoning, a shift from using words as weapons to embracing their healing power.

If we use our words as weapons seasoned with wisdom to do good work, we can transform conflicts into conversations, hatred into understanding, and indifference into compassion. Harnessing the power of speech, rooted in knowledge and intent, can change the narrative of our interactions and foster environments where growth, collaboration, and unity flourish. By making this conscious choice, we can redirect our society's trajectory toward positive change, one word at a time. Let this book invite all to introspect, evolve, and find that sacred space where words transform from battle tools to healing instruments, from weapons to wisdom.

In my silence, God's Word became a bridge between my anguish and hope, despair, and faith. I believe, fervently, that others too can harness this power, turning to the sacred scriptures not just as a refuge but as a guide, a compass pointing towards their true north.

I encourage you to embody biblical teachings actively. Ponder the passages; consider jotting them down, revisiting them, and rewriting them. Absorb their essence, immerse yourself in their wisdom, and let them serve as a sanctuary from the world's din, allowing God, The Logos, to take precedence in your heart and mind.

For anyone reading this, facing insurmountable challenges or drowning in the tumultuous waves of life's trials, know there is a lifeline awaiting you, as it did for me. When you find yourself lost, overwhelmed, or without words, remember the same '911' I dialed into - Psalm 119. This chapter, the longest in the Book of Psalms, is a testament to the transformative power of God's teachings. Each verse, rich in depth and wisdom, serves as a reminder of God's enduring love, guidance, and the boundless comfort in His word.

Psalm 119 isn't just a passage; it's a journey. It is a journey of meditation upon God's statutes, seeking understanding, and yearning for guidance in every step. Each stanza provides an anchor, a steadying force amidst life's storms. One can find comfort, strength, and direction by delving deep into its verses, meditating upon its truths, and internalizing its teachings.

As you navigate your life, with its peaks, valleys, joys, and sorrows, I encourage you to turn to Psalm 119. Let it be your '911', your emergency line to God's heart. And as you absorb its wisdom, may you also experience the transformative power of God's Word, finding a renewed purpose, a renewed spirit, and a path that leads to true peace and fulfillment.

Remember, in your moments of calm, in times of trial and tribulation, the divine lifeline is just a prayer away. Let God's Word light your path, and may you walk it with grace, faith, and unyielding strength.

May the insights and lessons from our time together remain with you, illuminating your path long after this book rests on your shelf.

I wholeheartedly believe and trust that your life will transform. Having prayed for my readers, I anticipate miraculous outcomes. I eagerly await your testimonies.

Please share your experiences with me at guirgisc@yahoo.com.

With gratitude and hope for our future,
Caroline Hanna Guirgis

Discussion Questions

Chapter 1 – Words as Weapons

1. How do the events described in this chapter highlight the impact and power of words as tools for harm and instruments for change?

2. Based on the encounters described in the chapter, how does prejudice manifest in different forms, and how do these forms intersect?

3. What is the significance of the author's interaction with Keisha, and how does it illustrate the complexity of bullying and the roles individuals can play within these dynamics?

4. How do external geopolitical events, like the Iran hostage situation, shape personal experiences and perceptions at a micro-level, and how does the author's Egyptian heritage become a focal point of misunderstanding and prejudice?

Chapter 2 - The Unlikely Warrior

1. The author describes a significant dichotomy between her behavior at home and her protective nature outside. What factors might have contributed to this dual identity? How does this dual nature reflect broader societal expectations and conditioning?

2. Respect and justice are central themes in this chapter. How does the author balance her inherent desire to treat individuals with respect while simultaneously confronting them on their unjust behaviors? Can one maintain respect for another while fiercely opposing their actions?

3. Passive aggressiveness is highlighted as a particularly challenging form of injustice. Why might this form of behavior be more damaging than overt aggression? How does the author's approach to addressing passive-aggressiveness emphasize the complexities of interpersonal relationships and communication?

4. The chapter touches on the author's internal struggles and vulnerabilities, especially when faced with covert prejudice. How does this internal battle challenge her identity as a defender against injustice? What does this reveal about the multifaceted nature of personal growth and resilience?

Chapter 3 - The Reflection and Reckoning

1. The author speaks of moments where she became more aggressive within her Christian communities, a place she expected to epitomize grace. Why do you think there was a heightened emotional response within these faith-based interactions compared to outside the community?

2. What are the dangers of placing heightened expectations on members within a close-knit or faith-based community? How do these expectations impact the relationships within the group?

3. Drawing parallels from the Tower of Babel story, how do you perceive the balance between the power of unified communication and the potential hazards of miscommunication? Can you relate this to contemporary issues?

4. Reflecting on the author's journey, how do unchecked emotions and a passion for justice and fairness potentially lead one astray from their intended path or beliefs?

Chapter 4 - Unleashing the Power

1. Words have been described as having the potential to both harm and heal. How does the author's journey of transformation reflect this dichotomy? Can you think of personal instances where words had a similar double-edged effect?

2. In the chapter, there's a mention of "mindfulness" in communication. What does it mean to communicate mindfully, and why is this essential in our relationships and interactions?

3. The author draws a connection between hubris (pride) and the creation of one's "Tower of Babel." How does unchecked pride influence our communication, and what are the potential consequences?

4. Reflecting on John's journey, how does the "Living Word" serve as a powerful tool for transformation and healing? How does his story emphasize the enduring nature of foundational teachings or experiences from our past?

Chapter 5 – The Unforeseen Redemption

1. The chapter speaks of the transformation of love into hatred within the bounds of marriage. What factors do you believe contribute to such drastic emotional shifts? How can individuals safeguard against allowing external influences and fleeting emotions to redefine the core of their relationships?

2. The potency of words, especially in expressions such as "I hate you," is explored. How do societal norms and personal experiences shape our understanding and reaction to such potent words? Can we employ strategies to communicate our feelings without resorting to such emotionally charged language?

3. Considering the power and influence of words, both positive and negative, in realms like childhood, marriage, and the sacred, how can individuals be more intentional and mindful about the words they choose to use? What role do personal introspection and spiritual practices, like engaging with scriptures or Psalms, play in refining our speech?

4. The chapter highlights the historical and societal evolution of curse words. How do you view the balance between the cathartic release some find in using profanity and the potential harm such words can cause? How can an understanding of linguistic, cultural, and historical influences on profanity inform our modern-day approach to communication?

Chapter 6 - Crafting a New Discourse:

1. How do you view the correlation between the Tower of Babel and the internet in terms of human ambition, unity, and division?

2. With the rapid advancement of digital technology and the internet, what ethical considerations are most pressing in today's digital age? How can individuals and societies strike a balance between harnessing the benefits of the Internet and addressing potential ethical dilemmas?

3. How do you think the internet has shaped the identity and worldview of younger generations, both positively and negatively? What roles should educational institutions play in equipping younger generations with the tools to navigate the digital world responsibly?

4. The chapter concludes with a call to promote positive content online. How feasible do you think this is given the vast and diverse nature of the internet? How can individuals, communities, and platforms encourage the creation and dissemination of uplifting and constructive content in the digital realm?

Chapter 7 – The Profound Power of Wyrd:

1. The chapter highlights the duality of words, emphasizing their ability to heal, connect, and hurt. Reflecting on your personal experiences, can you share a moment when words profoundly impacted you, either positively or negatively? How did this influence your perspective on the power of language?

2. Drawing parallels from the Tower of Babel story, in what ways do you think modern society showcases pride and self-glorification through language and communication? How can we promote humility and genuine connection in our increasingly digital and interconnected world?

3. The text delves into the concept of "negativity bias" and the evolutionary reasons behind it. How do you see this bias manifesting in today's media, personal interactions, or internal dialogue? What steps can individuals take to counteract this predisposition towards negativity?

4. Given the connection between our spiritual beliefs and how we use words, how can one's faith influence and guide healthier communication patterns? Can you think of any teachings or scriptures emphasizing the importance of thoughtful and empathetic speech?

Chapter 8 - Unveiling Parallels

1. The chapter parallels the Tower of Babel story and the modern internet era. How do these parallels illuminate humanity's ongoing communication tools and aspirations challenges? In what ways might our current society benefit from heeding the lessons of the Tower of Babel story?

2. As described in the chapter, the Logos is a philosophical and theological concept transcending linguistic confines. How do various spiritual and philosophical traditions understand and interpret the idea of the "Living Word"? How might an individual's understanding of Logos shape their perspective on the power and responsibility of words?

3. The Word, in its various forms, can be seen as a "double-edged sword," capable of both profound positive impact and potential harm. How do individuals navigate this duality in daily communication? How can we become more mindful and responsible custodians of the words we choose to use?

4. The chapter touches upon the transformative nature of encountering and being overcome by divine power. How do individuals from different spiritual backgrounds describe and understand this profound experience? How can such experiences influence an individual's relationship with themselves, others, and the universe?

Chapter 9 – The Liturgy of the Word

1. The chapter vividly depicts the liturgical experience—from incense aroma to hymns' resonance. How do sensory elements contribute to liturgical worship's spiritual depth and richness? Do you believe engaging multiple senses can enhance one's connection to the divine?

2. Repetition in the liturgy, as described in the chapter, acts as an anchor, embedding sacred truths deeply within believers. How might what seems to be rote repetition transform into a profound spiritual experience over time? Can you think of other areas in life where repetition brings deeper understanding or significance?

3. The Liturgy of the Word in the Coptic Church emphasizes passive hearing and an active encounter with God's living Word. How does the liturgy facilitate this active engagement with scripture? What is the significance of the congregation's role, especially with elements like the singing of the "Alleluia" before the Gospel reading?

4. The chapter mentions the Holy Spirit as the "living breath" that animates the words and rituals of the liturgy. How does the presence of the Holy Spirit transform the liturgy from a mere formality into a vibrant experience of the Divine? Can you share personal experiences or observations where you felt the Holy Spirit's transformative power during a religious ceremony or ritual?

Chapter 10 – From Weapons to Wisdom

1. The chapter emphasizes the potency of words, especially for those who resonate with the love language of "Words of Affirmation." How have words influenced your understanding of self-worth and value, and how do these shape your interactions with others?

2. he author shares a personal perspective on the vulnerability of being sensitive to words. Do you believe this vulnerability can be both a strength and a weakness? Discuss situations where sensitivity to words has positively and negatively affected relationships.

3. Imagine a society predominantly built on positive affirmations, as outlined in the chapter. How would such a society differ from our current one regarding mental health, interpersonal relationships, and community cohesion? Are there potential drawbacks to such a society?

4. The chapter envisions a future where consistent positive communication becomes the norm, leading to a more emotionally intelligent and empathetic generation. How can we actively work towards creating this environment in our homes, schools, and communities? Discuss the practical steps and potential challenges.

Chapter 11 – Transforming Dialogue

1. The chapter delves into humans' resistance towards surrendering control to a Higher Power. How does this human need for autonomy and validation compare with the guidance offered by God's Word? How can one reconcile the tension between self-assertion and spiritual surrender?

2. Daily, we follow societal norms, rules, and conventions while sometimes neglecting spiritual tenets. What factors influence our decision to adhere to specific rules while questioning or disregarding others? How does societal conditioning play a role in shaping our priorities?

3. The power of hearing, mainly through music or repeated phrases, is highlighted in the chapter. How does this influence our perception and connection to God's Word? Can auditory resonance strengthen faith or improve our understanding of spiritual teachings?

4. The chapter touches upon the tendency of humans to blame God during adversities and misunderstand His intentions. How can individuals better differentiate between human imperfections and the actual teachings of God's Word? How does one's belief system influence their interpretation of divine intent and challenges in life?

Chapter 12 – Transforming Destiny

1. Consider the foundational beliefs you hold about God and spirituality. What are their origins? Are they beliefs passed down from family or religious figures, personal experiences, or a combination? Reflect on how these beliefs shape your interactions with the Divine and others.

2. Recall a moment in your life when you felt the teachings of any scripture or spiritual text come alive through someone's actions. How did that impact your understanding or appreciation of that teaching? Reflect on how you might embody these teachings in your daily life, moving beyond mere reverence of the text to actual lived experiences.

3. Think about moments when you've felt overwhelmed or in conflict. How often did you resort to using words as weapons or defense mechanisms? Reflect on the transformative power of silence and introspection. How can you cultivate moments of silence in your daily routine, allowing for a deeper connection with your inner self and the Divine?

4. Spend some time meditating on Psalm 119 or any other spiritual text that resonates with you. How do its teachings align with your current life circumstances? Reflect on its verses, seeking wisdom and guidance for challenges you might be facing. How can this scripture serve as a constant '911' or lifeline for you during turbulent times?

About the Author

Caroline Hanna Guirgis is an author with a heart for wisdom. Caroline's path as a writer is intertwined with her voyage as a compassionate human, making her books not just a literary experience but a reflection of her soul. An avid reader from a young age, Caroline's passion for literature was never limited to mere consumption. She felt the pull of words, the allure of stories, and their profound impact on people. This fascination ultimately led her to delve deep into the study of words in this publication. It's not just about semantics or lexicon but about how words shape thoughts, mold emotions, and can either wound hearts or heal them.

Beyond her identity as an author, Caroline is deeply rooted in her commitment to nurturing the next generation. Working in a private Christian school, she doesn't just view her role as an educator but as a guiding light. Every student under her care isn't just another name on a roll; they are individuals with dreams, challenges, and potential. Those who know Caroline speak volumes about her unwavering commitment to family and friends. They paint a picture of a woman whose love knows no bounds and whose dedication to those she cares about is inspiring. Like everything else she does, this book will be a testament to her journey, her beliefs, and her undying passion for making a difference, one word at a time.

Printed in the United States
by Baker & Taylor Publisher Services